A SKYSCRAPER Story

A SKYSCRAPER Story

BY CHARLOTTE WILCOX
with a foreword by Cesar Pelli

PHOTOGRAPHS BY JERRY BOUCHER

 Carolrhoda Books, Inc./Minneapolis

Special thanks to Lloyd P. Johnson, Chairman and Chief Executive Officer, and John R. Kerr, Assistant Vice President of Corporate Communications of Norwest Corporation; Paul Cossette, Senior Project Manager, Mark Schmidt, Project Engineer, and Bud Peck, Corporate Services of Mortenson/Schal; Jon Pickard, Senior Associate of Cesar Pelli and Associates; and Laurence Burns, Project Architect of Kendall/Heaton Associates, Incorporated.

The photograph on pages 12-13 courtesy of Mark Chulik, and the photograph on page 14 courtesy of Hines Interests Limited Partnership.

Norwest Center is a development of NWC Limited Partnership, which includes Hines Interests Limited Partnership, Norwest Corporation, and ARICO America Realestate Investment Company.

LIBRARY OF CONGRESS CATALOGING-IN-PUBLICATION DATA

Wilcox, Charlotte.
A skyscraper story / by Charlotte Wilcox, with a foreword by Cesar Pelli ; photographs by Jerry Boucher.
p.   cm.
Summary: Describes the building of Norwest Center, a fifty-seven story skyscraper in Minneapolis.
ISBN 0-87614-392-3
1. Skyscrapers—Design and construction—Juvenile literature.
[1. Skyscrapers. 2. Building.] I. Boucher, Jerry, 1941-   ill.
II. Title.
TH1615.W54   1990
690—dc20   90-1836
                                                                                    CIP
                                                                                    AC

Manufactured in the United States of America

1 2 3 4 5 6 7 8 9 99 98 97 96 95 94 93 92 91 90

To Dad and Charles

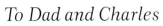

Foreword

by Cesar Pelli

Architecture is a complex art. Unlike painting or sculpture, it is greatly affected by the conditions around it: site, technology, client, and city. This is not a weakness of architecture, but one of its strengths. Changes constantly challenge architects to recheck and redefine their ideas if they want to continue to create successful buildings. Architecture is a social art.

For Norwest Center, as with all of our buildings, we started by finding out what kind of architecture the site, the client, and the users needed. We designed a unique building in response to these requirements. I say *we* because, although I led the design, architecture is produced by teams of architects, engineers, and consultants.

Before beginning the design for Norwest Center, we took long walks, exploring the city to get a feel for its special qualities. We saw that many Minneapolis buildings are warm beige, a good color for long winters, and that many of them have windows arranged in vertical ribbons. We also sensed in Minneapolis a strong but quiet feeling of pride. With these measurable and immeasurable qualities in mind, we were ready to begin our design.

A building is a piece of a city, so its design must be based on how it will affect the city. We built a model of downtown Minneapolis to explore several possible building forms for Norwest Center. We tried tall and short buildings of different shapes, and we ended up proposing a design for a building that is somewhat shorter than Minneapolis's tallest building, the IDS Center, but with a distinctive shape. We felt that our design was beautiful and would fit in with the look of the city. Our clients agreed.

In addition to building a pleasing form, we had to satisfy functional and structural requirements. The elevator and the structure were built to be efficient for the 57-story building; an increase in the building's height would have noticeably increased their expense. Also, the floors were built to be the right size for efficient space planning. Setbacks, which narrow the building as it rises, were added to make Norwest Center a more elegant addition to the city skyline.

While the engineers were working on building structure and efficiency, we designed the outside of the building. We chose Kasota, a local Minnesota limestone with a beautiful ocher beige color. To make the building seem sunnier, we included a great deal of white trim in the building's piers, setbacks, and window mullions. On the top edges of the setbacks, we used shiny gold-colored ornaments (we call them finials) that catch the light and sparkle. Most of the white and gold is at the tower's top, which glows with the smallest bit of sunshine.

Other techniques were used at the lower levels of Norwest Center that represent the care with which it was designed. A sky bridge, which we designed in collaboration with artist Siah Armajani of Minneapolis, creates a glowing space at its center, making the bridge itself a place worthy of visit. It was also our goal to create a "people place," so we designed the rotunda—a grand public space with a large skylight. Inside, we decorated by hanging six large brass chandeliers and by using other objects saved from the bank building that had burned down on Thanksgiving Day in 1982. These objects connect Norwest Center to the history of its site.

In Norwest Center we have tried to build a high-quality building that fits in the city of Minneapolis and makes it a better place. When a building is finished and one feels that one's goals have been achieved, as we feel in this case, nothing is as fulfilling and rewarding as architecture.

The story of the skyscraper is an American story because the skyscraper was born in America. It is a story of steel and concrete because skyscrapers could not have been built without steel and concrete. It is a story of invention because dozens of new machines and materials had to be invented before skyscrapers could be built. Most of all, it is a story of cooperation because the thousands of people needed to build a skyscraper must depend on each other to turn an architect's plans into a safe, useful building.

Most skyscrapers have names. The skyscraper in this story is called Norwest Center and is owned by NWC Limited Partnership. The story of how Norwest Center was built is in many ways the story of all skyscrapers. Like people, each new skyscraper is different from any other, but all have many things in common.

Two features make a building a skyscraper. To be a skyscraper, a building must be very tall. Most modern skyscrapers are 20 to 70 stories high, and the tallest are over 100 stories. Norwest Center has 57 stories, making it 772½ feet tall. A skyscraper must also be built around a frame made of steel, or steel and concrete. This **skeleton frame** is strong enough to support the weight of a very tall building.

The skeleton frame in this picture is already 14 stories high—and no walls are up yet. You can see that the building would stand strong even if it never had walls. The skeleton frame will be completely hidden after the outer walls are in place. The outer walls, called **curtain walls**, don't hold the building up—they only separate the inside of the building from the outside.

This skyscraper story begins with a fire. A beautiful old skyscraper was badly burned in a fire that blazed on Thanksgiving Day in 1982. The building was damaged beyond repair, so it had to be torn down. Because it had been built in such a good location, the owners wanted to build a new, taller sky-scraper in the same spot. Before the old building was torn down, some of the lights and other **fixtures** were saved to become part of the new building. But more than two years would pass before actual planning for Norwest Center would begin.

Before a skyscraper is built, certain ques-tions must be answered. How will the new skyscraper affect the people who already live and work near it? Will its shadow keep sun-light from shining into windows nearby? Will dangerous drafts of wind blow between it and other skyscrapers? Many experts help answer these questions.

How a fire over 100 years ago got the modern skyscraper off the ground

In 1871, a large part of Chicago, Illinois, went up in flames. The fire burned out of control for two days, ruining many buildings, including the homes of 100,000 people. Chicago had to be rebuilt.

Large apartment buildings were needed to house the many people whose homes had burned. Office buildings, stores, factories, and warehouses were needed all at once.

Many famous architects went to Chicago to use their new designs and techniques to rebuild the city. The world's first true skyscraper—built on a steel skeleton frame—went up in 1885. Many other skyscrapers were built, and this new style of architecture became known as the Chicago School. Some of the tallest buildings in the world are still located in Chicago.

This is the scale model made by the architect from cardboard, glue, and other art materials. It is about as tall as an average sixth grader.

By 1985, the people of Minneapolis decided that a new skyscraper, Norwest Center, could be built. Then it had to be designed and carefully planned. An architect with experience in building skyscrapers was hired. He looked at studies of the neighborhood, skyline, and soil. He found out how much money the owner planned to spend. He studied the area where the skyscraper would be located to choose the building materials that would be available and that would fit in with the look of the city. His job was to design the most beautiful, useful building possible with the money and materials available.

The architect's team produced about 600 drawings, called **blueprints**, showing every detail of construction. The team included engineers who studied many factors that affect the construction of every large building.

The **dead load** is the total weight of all the materials used to construct a building, along with all the items that will be attached to the inside of the building. A weight is calculated for every pound of concrete and steel, every foot of wire and pipe, every door and window, and every wall and ceiling.

The total weight of all the people who are expected to be inside a building at any one time is called the **live load**. Besides the people, a building must be able to support all the fresh air, water, and movable furniture that people will need while inside the skyscraper. Even though it's invisible, air does have weight and puts stress on a building. Rain, snow, and ice are also part of the live load.

The **wind load** is the stress that wind puts on a building. Weather at the top of a skyscraper can be different from weather at the bottom. Engineers study weather reports to learn how the winds are likely to blow at the top of a skyscraper.

Earthquakes, hurricanes, and other environmental factors must be considered in areas where they might occur. Norwest Center is located in an area that can be very hot in summer and very cold in winter. Because building materials have a tendency to stretch in hot weather and shrink in cold weather, Norwest Center was designed to allow for these environmental factors.

Designing the building took about a year to complete—but the planning was far from done. The architect's drawings were used to create over 10,000 more detailed drawings, called shop drawings. These were used in the next stage of planning—the construction schedule.

The **general contractor** is a company that is in charge of the building process. Its job is to coordinate the work of **subcontractors**—companies that work on separate tasks—and suppliers—companies that supply materials. About 50 different subcontractors, along with over 500 suppliers, worked on Norwest Center.

General contractors also decide how much of each kind of building material will be needed.

**H**ere is part of the "shopping list" for Norwest Center:

16,500 tons of steel
6 tons of screws
3.5 tons of nails
7 acres of stone (enough to cover 64 basketball courts)
8 acres of glass (enough to cover 12 football fields)
30 acres of steel decking (enough to cover 6 city blocks)
80 acres of drywall (enough to cover a cornfield half a mile long and a quarter of a mile wide)
15 acres of insulation (enough to cover the walls of 1,000 classrooms)
33,000 cubic yards of concrete (enough to fill 58 railroad cars)
150 miles of electrical wire (enough to stretch from New York to Boston)
30 miles of plumbing pipe
4,000 doors on 12,000 hinges
500,000 nuts and bolts

Like most skyscrapers, Norwest Center was built in the middle of a large city. It took a lot of planning to get all the materials and hundreds of workers to the site without creating traffic jams. Once all the planning was completed, building could begin.

In August 1986, bulldozers and backhoes began digging the basement of the new building. Cranes lifted large pieces of the old basement to be hauled away. Soon a huge hole, the size of half a city block, had been dug.

Machines continued to dig and dig and dig some more. Tons of earth from the hole was piled into dump trucks and hauled away. Before the digging stopped, the hole reached 50 feet below street level, exposing a layer of solid rock, called **bedrock**. The huge skyscraper would rest on this rock.

As soon as the hole reached bedrock, workers began preparing the bottom level of the building. They cut holes into the bedrock surface for **footings**, the structures that Norwest Center stands on. The holes were filled with concrete reinforced with steel rods to make it stronger. Footings are especially important because they support the entire building.

Steel rods sticking up from the top of the footings fastened the **columns** to the footings. The columns stand on top of the footings and support the rest of the skeleton frame.

The skeleton frame

Columns rise from the footings to the rooftops above. They bear most of the weight of a building. The narrower columns are made of steel, and the wider columns, called supercolumns, are made of concrete reinforced with steel. Norwest Center has four supercolumns—two on each side.

At each story, the columns are connected by steel **girders**, which form the outer frame of the building. Each story is crossed with lighter steel **beams**, which support each floor.

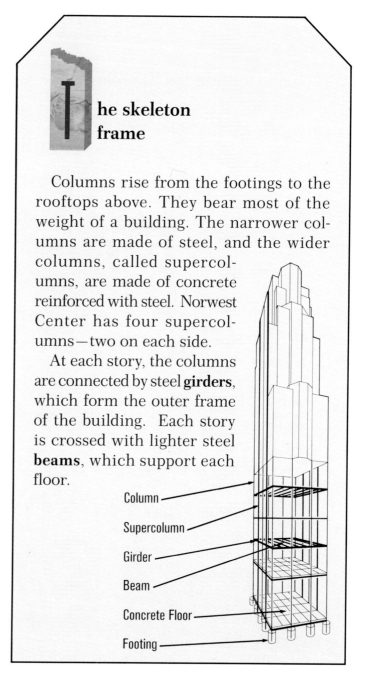

Column
Supercolumn
Girder
Beam
Concrete Floor
Footing

As soon as the concrete in the footings was **cured**, so it would be strong enough to hold the weight of the skeleton frame, the iron workers began their work. The steel columns, girders, and beams were fitted together, bolted in place, then welded at the joints to become the skeleton frame of the skyscraper. Workers and cranes teamed up to put the pieces together, and the skeleton frame rose higher and higher.

Of all the machines used in building sky-scrapers, the cranes are among the most important. These powerful lifting machines carry materials to the upper stories. Without cranes, skyscrapers would be difficult to build.

When the work on Norwest Center was at ground level, truck cranes did all the lifting. Truck cranes move easily on wheels. As the building's skeleton grew out to the street and up from the ground, there was no longer any room for the truck cranes. Two tower cranes then arrived to do the rest of the lifting.

Tower cranes are eight stories tall, but they do not move on wheels. Two large holes were left in the floor of each story for the cranes. At first, the tower cranes sat on the ground, with the operator's cage about level with the eighth story. When the framework for the first eight stories was completed, a special **hydraulic** lifting device at the bottom of each crane raised it higher. Tower cranes can move only four stories at a time. At Norwest Center, the tower cranes were raised 12 times before they reached the top. After the skeleton frame was completed, the cranes were taken away, and the two holes in each story were filled. The tower cranes had lifted thousands of tons of steel, concrete, and other materials for Norwest Center.

Another lifting device used was the **hoist**, a boxlike cage that moves on steel framework on the outside of a skyscraper. A motor on top of the cage turns gears that pull the cage up and down. Two hoists were operated during construction of Norwest Center. The hoists were used to move workers, tools, and materials up and down the building as it grew taller. By the time the framework was completed to the 57th story, the hoists offered quite a ride!

It took 40 iron workers 12 months to complete Norwest Center's skeleton frame—but before they got very far, the cement workers started their biggest job of all.

The cement workers began pouring concrete for the supercolumns and floors as winter 1986 was setting in. First iron workers built the columns up a few stories at a time. Then the cement workers began filling the hollow columns with high-strength concrete.

The steel beams in the supercolumns are flexible, so they bend just a little in the wind. The concrete is heavy and very strong. Steel and concrete work together to make skyscrapers just strong enough, just heavy enough, and just flexible enough to be very sturdy.

The concrete used in the supercolumns was made to harden within a short period of time—about two days—allowing crews to work without waiting for the concrete to be cured completely. By the time the iron workers were ready to put up more stories, the concrete in the supercolumns below was strong enough to support them.

After a few stories of columns, girders, and beams were finished, work began on the last part of the skyscraper's skeleton frame—the floors. Steel beams, crossing from one side of the building to the other, support the surface of each floor. The beams are covered with thin sheets of steel decking, which supports the drying concrete for each floor.

Next the concrete that was to become the actual floor of each story was poured over the steel decking. The concrete used for floors is a different type from that used for supercolumns. It cures slowly—for almost two months—but is safe to walk on in just one day because of the steel decking underneath it. Cement workers have to move quickly to level the concrete before it hardens.

Steel and concrete are the only materials that can be used for a skeleton frame's columns, beams, and floors. Many different materials can be used for a skyscraper's curtain walls, though, because curtain walls do not have to support any weight. The architect was free to choose materials that would make the outside of Norwest Center beautiful and the inside sunny and comfortable.

Norwest Center's outer "skin" is made from three materials—limestone and marble, which are types of stone, and glass. In this picture, you can see all three materials as they were being attached. The curtain walls have not yet been attached to the upper stories. The stories in the middle of the picture have only the gray glass attached. The stories near the bottom of the picture have the stone wall panels in place.

Below: *Glass panels are being swung into place by a crane.*

Next workers placed sheets of **insulation** over the areas of curtain wall that would be covered with stone. You can see the limestone already in place below the workers. They worked from a special platform, called a **swing stage**.

While the iron workers and cement workers were erecting the upper stories of Norwest Center, many new workers began arriving to start working inside.

A skyscraper must be safe for the people who will work or live in it. That means fireproofing, among other things. Ladders and hoses from fire trucks can only reach the first few stories of a skyscraper, so fire fighters must work from the inside if fires break out.

Serious fires are rare in skyscrapers because they are built of steel and concrete, which do not burn. The only things that burn in a skyscraper are the furnishings inside. While steel beams can't burn, they will melt or buckle if they get too hot, which could cause a floor to cave in. To keep this from happening, the steel beams in Norwest Center were sprayed with a special coating to protect them from heat.

**W**hat happens if fire starts in a skyscraper

1. Water stored in special pipes above the ceiling tiles is sprayed through sprinklers near the fire.

2. Huge fans come on, sucking air out of the story where the fire started. Fire needs air to burn.

3. Elevator doors automatically close. Elevators are programmed to go to a story chosen beforehand by the fire department.

4. Stairway doors, which are usually electrically locked, open.

By the end of 1987, about 400 workers were at the site every day. They worked for over a year before they were done.

The inside workers brought new materials with them. Water pipes were crisscrossed under each floor. Hundreds of heating and cooling units were installed to control air temperature throughout the building. The lower stories began to fill up with materials, tools, supplies, and people.

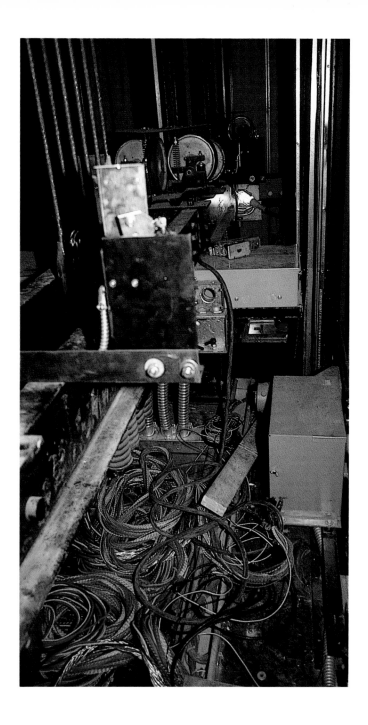

Left: *Everything in this picture is used to operate one elevator car. This equipment controls the movement of the elevator and brings in fresh air and a telephone line in case of emergency.*

Opposite: *These men are working in the doorway to an elevator car.*

Electrical and mechanical crews are responsible for installing the systems that will make a skyscraper work: electrical, plumbing, heating, cooling, ventilation, transportation, and communication. The elevators were among the first things installed in Norwest Center by one of the mechanical crews.

Skyscrapers could never have been built without elevators. People would be spending too much time and energy getting to the upper stories by climbing stairs. It would take at least 20 minutes to get to the top of Norwest Center by stairs. An elevator takes 40 seconds, traveling 1,200 feet per minute, to get to the top story.

Norwest Center has 31 elevators, but only 1 of them goes all the way from the very bottom to the very top. Like most modern skyscrapers, Norwest Center uses a computerized system to control the elevators, so people can be moved up and down the building as safely and as quickly as possible.

 ## ow the elevators work

The elevator car moves up and down by cables attached to the top of the car. Each car has several cables, and each cable is strong enough to support a car by itself. The cables move around a large wheel, called a sheave, at the top of the elevator shaft. An electric motor beside the sheave makes it turn, pulling the cables to move the car. The cables are attached at the opposite end to very heavy pieces of iron, called counterweights. The counterweights are about the same weight as an elevator car full of passengers. As the weights are pulled down by gravity, they help pull the car up. The counterweights also help keep the car from dropping too fast when it is on its way down. In addition, each car is equipped with computerized brakes for smooth stops.

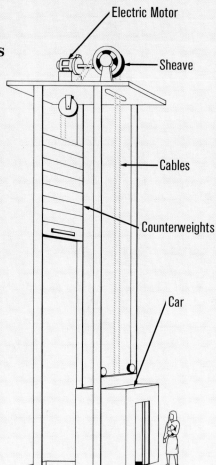

Electric Motor

Sheave

Cables

Counterweights

Car

The mechanical crews continued their work by installing the heating and cooling systems. This shiny metal box, which looks like a chimney, is part of the **ductwork**. The ductwork runs up and down the entire building, with openings to every story. Fresh air—cool in summer and warm in winter—is piped through some of the ductwork. Other ducts return old, used air to the outside.

The mechanical crews installed almost 30 miles of plumbing pipe inside the walls and ceilings of Norwest Center. Some water goes to restrooms and kitchens, some is used for fire protection, and some for air conditioning.

Color-coded wire was used for the electrical and telephone systems in the building. Different colors were used so the electricians could tell which wire went where as 150 miles of wire was strung throughout the building. The wires were then threaded through special metal piping, called **conduits**, to protect them from damage and fire.

Below: *These huge pipes carry thousands of gallons of water up and down the building every day.*

The next crews to start work were the finishing crews. Their job was to convert each open story into rooms with all the features—hallways, doors, closets, ceilings, lights, and other fixtures—that are needed to make them comfortable and useful.

First metal wires were attached to the underside of the steel decking that formed the floor of the story above it. These wires would hold the framework that would become the finished ceiling. Next the ceiling was criss-crossed with the metal framework that is needed to hold the ceiling tiles.

Some large areas were divided into rooms. Walls for the rooms were created by installing upright metal frames, called **studs**. They were held in place by metal tracks bolted into the concrete floor. The studs were then covered with sheets of **drywall**, which became the walls of the rooms.

By this time, the iron workers had completed the skeleton frame, and the cement workers were just finishing their work on the highest stories. As the curtain walls rose higher and higher, some finishing touches were completed at the roof levels.

Left: *A small area of a roof is tested before the whole roof is waterproofed. It is coated with rubber, then flooded with water to make sure it won't leak. After it passes the test, the entire roof is coated.*

The roofs were covered with steel decking and concrete similar to that used for the floors. Then they were waterproofed with rubber roofing material, so nothing would leak into the more than one million square feet of office rooms below. Finally the roofs were covered with beautiful brick tiles.

Even when the finishing crews were well underway, the inside of Norwest Center looked rough and bare—until the decorating crews began their work. These wallpaper hangers, painters, woodworkers, and carpet layers add the finishing touches to every area of a building.

They turned this ▼

into this. ►

The decorating crews covered up almost everything the iron workers, cement workers, mechanical crews, electrical crews, and finishing crews had done. They used materials that would make Norwest Center a pleasant and comfortable place.

The decorating crews added soft lighting and pleasant colors for large, open areas with many workers. They painted, wallpapered, and installed carpet and wood floors. They made cabinets for the smaller offices, and added **molding** around the doorways, windows, and where the walls meet the floors.

The finishing and decorating crews continued working after all the other crews were done. They installed 46,000 electrical outlets, 20,000 light fixtures, 4,000 doors on 12,000 hinges, 80 acres of drywall, and 25 acres of floor covering. That would be enough material to complete 700 single-family homes!

Scale model of Norwest Center made by the architect. It is 4 feet tall.

Norwest Center was finally completed in the spring of 1989—five years after planning began and almost three years after the first backhoe started digging.

The architect had designed a beautiful building that would be safe and useful. The general contractor had brought all the different materials and people together. The iron workers, cement workers, mechanical crews, and electrical crews had made the skyscraper strong and safe. The finishing and decorating crews had made it beautiful and useful.

*The completed Norwest Center
skyscraper. It is 772½ feet tall.*

Altogether, over 3,000 people worked on
Norwest Center. Each crew, from the architect's team to the last decorating crews, completed an important part of the building.
Together they made it work.

GLOSSARY

beams: straight, horizontal bars of steel that support the floors of a skyscraper

bedrock: the solid layer of rock beneath the soil

blueprints: copies of the architect's plans for a building that are printed on a special machine

columns: tall pillars that support part of a building and transfer the weight of a skyscraper to the footings

conduits: pipes or tubes that protect electrical wires and cables

cured: hardened properly and completely over a period of time

curtain walls: the outer walls of a skyscraper, which do not bear any weight

dead load: the total weight of construction materials and attached interior accessories of a building

drywall: a building material made of sheets of plaster covered with paper

ductwork: a system of pipes or tubes through which air is moved to different parts of a building

fixtures: equipment, such as lights or sinks, that is attached to a building

footings: bases for columns that distribute the weight of a building

general contractor: the company responsible for overseeing all phases of a construction project

girders: straight bars of steel that are the main supports for a building

hoist: a large, usually open elevator that moves on the outside of a skyscraper

hydraulic: operated by water or other liquid under pressure

insulation: material, placed between the inner and outer walls of a building, used to keep out extreme temperatures

live load: the total weight of the air, water, movable furniture, and all the people who may be in a building at one time

molding: decorative strips of wood or other material used as edging on the interior of a building

skeleton frame: the internal supporting structure of a skyscraper

studs: upright posts to which a wall is attached

subcontractor: a company working for a general contractor on a specific phase of construction

swing stage: a temporary platform for construction workers to stand on when they are working above ground level

wind load: the effect that wind has on a building